THE ARROW PRAYER

A PRAYER FOR ALL CHRISTIANS

SAINT SHENOUDA PRESS

THE ARROW PRAYER

A PRAYER FOR ALL CHRISTIANS

By: Fr Anthony St Shenouda

ST SHENOUDA PRESS
SYDNEY, AUSTRALIA
2024

The Arrow Prayer: A Prayer for all Christians
By: Fr Anthony St Shenouda

_____

St Shenouda Press
8419 Putty Rd,
Putty, NSW, 2330
Sydney, Australia

www.stshenoudapress.com

ISBN 13: 978-1-7635450-4-5

_____

CONTENTS

INTRODUCTION

"Rejoice always, pray without ceasing, in everything give thanks; for this is the will of God in Christ Jesus for you." (1 Thessalonians 5:16-18)

When we read this verse, we seem to concentrate on rejoicing always then we skip to giving thanks and we often leave out the *pray without ceasing* part. This is mostly because we think of praying without ceasing as a command to the monks and nuns, not to a layperson who lives in the world. It is very clear in these verses that praying without ceasing is a command to laypeople, as much as rejoicing and giving thanks. I hope it is obvious that when St Paul was writing this epistle he was not writing it to monks. In fact, monasticism started at least 250 years after this epistle was written, further establishing laypersons as its target audience.

We can also assume when we read these verses, that when St Paul commanded the church in Thessaloniki to pray without ceasing, he assumed that it was possible for the whole church to fulfill this commandment. Otherwise, if it was not achievable he would not have commanded it.

Furthermore, praying without ceasing was not only the teaching of St Paul. Jesus in the gospel of St Luke taught the parable of the persistent widow who tirelessly asked the judge to give her justice against her adversary and the judge only gave her justice because of her persistence. St Luke starts this parable with this sentence: "Then He spoke a parable to them, that men *always ought to pray and not lose heart*" (Luke 18:1). Again, Jesus was not talking to monks or nuns but to farmers, fishermen, tax collectors and people from all walks of life.

This is the way the church understood these verses in later centuries, as we will discover throughout this book. Praying without ceasing is a command for all Christians from all walks of life. Working fulltime in any discipline does not excuse us from fulfilling this commandment. In case I have lost you already, ("easy for a monk to say") I hope to further explain what I mean with some practical applications throughout the book.

The Jesus Prayer:

In recent times, the practice of continuous prayer has been synonymous with the Jesus Prayer. All recent publications on the topic of prayer and particularly continuous prayer speak solely of the practice of the Jesus Prayer as practiced in the byzantine tradition, with special influence from Mount Athos. We owe this revival of the practice of the Jesus prayer to the publication of the book, *The Way of a Pilgrim*, which was written early in the twentieth century and translated to multiple languages very soon after. *The way of a pilgrim* narrates the story of a monk who wonders the Siberian wilderness in quest for the true practice of continuous prayer.

In this book I attempt to approach the topic differently. I will present the practice of continuous prayers as recorded in the literature and practices in the life of the Coptic Orthodox church, traditionally known as the Arrow Prayer.

As we will discover, the Jesus Prayer was very well known and widely used very early on by the early Christians. It was one of the ways that early Coptic Christians practiced continuous prayer, yet not as an exclusive prayer, but as a part of the larger tradition of the Arrow prayer.

To date, there have been very little publications that deal with this topic and I hope this book will bring to light this practice and hopefully answer the misconceptions that some readers might have.

What Is The Arrow Prayer?

The arrow prayer has no specific definition by any of the early church fathers or any ancient or contemporary text. After reading many of the sources that deal with the topic of prayer and specifically continuous prayer, I have put together a definition that closely outlines the main parameters of the prayer.

> A short prayer that is prayed by monks and laity, its content can be inspired from a verse from the bible or a personal prayer that is repeated throughout the day while practising their day to day activities.

This definition has three distinct elements that set it apart from any other mode of prayer. These three elements are:

1. A short prayer that is prayed by monks and laity.
2. The formula for the prayer can be inspired from a verse of the bible or a personal prayer.
3. It is repeated throughout the day while practicing your day to day activities.

In each of the following three chapters I will expand on each of these elements, giving examples from some of the ancient and not so ancient texts where it was used in this manner, as well as monastic writings, archeological finds, and liturgical prayers. Doing so, I hope to bring to light an ancient mode of prayer that has been in practice in the Coptic Church since its inception. Before I do that, it is important to give some background information and definitions of terms that will come up later in the book.

Where Did The Name Come From?

The name 'Arrow Prayer,' given to this method of prayer, is not as old as we think. The oldest recorded reference to this name comes from the twentieth century interview with a number of monks and bishops, in which they call the prayer *el salah el sahmya.*

Nevertheless, the practice of short continuous prayers has always been referred to in terms of war and arrows.

The earliest of these attestations is found in the writings of Evagrius, when he refers to continuous prayer as "an arrow shot from the saint by knowledge and reason and faith. And it wounds the spirits hostile to God to *destroy and overthrow them*". Later on, St Augustine describes the prayer practice of the monks of Egypt in this way: "The brethren in Egypt are reported to have very frequent prayers... very brief and sudden like a dart" Abba Palamon also taught St Pachomious the practice of continuous prayer at the beginning of his monastic life by praying the rule of the synaxis, "not counting the dart like [prayers] we make so as not to be defaulters, since we are commanded to pray without ceasing". Abba Palamon here notes that he learned this prayer from the fathers before him.

The most vivid story that depicts the use of short prayers as arrows comes from the life of a seventh century saint, St John the Hegumen of Scetes. In the *Life,* he narrates that the demons once appeared to an elder named Youanis, who used to practice unceasing prayer during the day and night and while he was doing his handiwork. One day, the devil appeared to him with a body that had been pierced with arrows saying: "stop, stop fighting me! I will not bother you again!" Abba Youanis continued:

> I said to him: 'and what are these on your body?'
> He said: 'these are arrows.'
> I said to him: 'who did all this to you'
> He said: 'you are the one'
> I said to him: 'and how did I do this to you?'
> He said to me: 'every time you stand up to pray, one of these pierces my body'

We see from these attestations that while the name was never given to the prayer until the twentieth century, yet the practice of short continuous prayers which defines the arrow prayer was always referred to as an arrow.

What Is The Formula?

Christianity did not start in a vacuum, but it was affected by the culture it grew in. Therefore, to understand what the formula is, we need to understand that when Christianity started, orality was predominant. Books were not as readily available as today, simply because they were very expensive. Thus, people had to rely on their memory to recall information.

To be able to memorise and retain information, you need to use many formulas. Not to use a formula to remember something was a waste of time, as it could not be remembered. It was merely a passing thought rather than an abiding knowledge.

Therefore, the formula was, and in many ways still is, the building block of memory. This was true in the context of composing poetry, schooling, and simply, in everyday activities that required memory.

Books, as I mentioned were a very expensive possession. The bible as a book was no exception and many Christians could not afford to keep their own copy. Hence, they did what the social norm dictates, they memorised large parts of the scripture. To do so, they had to memorise and repeat a large number of key verses or formulas from the bible.

The formula is therefore a phrase which comes from a verse of the bible or a saying of one of the church fathers; repeating it throughout the day makes up the arrow prayer. There was no specific method preferred over the other formulas, but it was simply any bible verse or edifying verse of the fathers. We know from the early text that even what came to be known as the 'Jesus Prayer' was not a preferred formula over the other formulas.

Reading the desert fathers, we learn that we don't have to invoke the name of Jesus to pray to Jesus. We can pray to Jesus by simply remembering God through the invocation of the psalms.

One of the examples comes from the seventh century monks, saints Barsanuphius and John. When St John was asked if it was necessary to "invoke the name of God" while we are around people, he replied:

> "When one is alone, one should recite the psalms and pray with one's mouth and one's heart. However when one is in the market place or with other people, it is not necessary to recite the psalms with one's mouth, but only with one's mind"

Therefore reciting the psalms was considered by St John as invoking the name of God.

The only incident the arrow prayer was reduced to one formula was in the writings of John Cassian. In his tenth conference, Abba Isaac advises St John to practice continuous prayer by using only one formula from (psalm 70:1):

> The formula for this discipline and prayer that you are seeking, then, shall be presented to you. Every monk who longs for the continual awareness of God should be in the habit of meditating on it ceaselessly in his heart… this, then, is the devotional formula proposed to you as absolutely necessary for possessing the perpetual awareness of God: "O God, incline unto my aid; O Lord, make haste to help me"

It is clear from the rest of the conference that this is not the normal practice of the prayer, but it was a way of keeping the mind from distraction while praying by remaining focused on one prayer.

Prayer Is Warfare To The Last Breath

On a more personal note, the practice of the arrow prayer or any other mode of prayer is a struggle that we must undertake every time we pray. I have asked myself many times, *"Why is it so hard to always pray? Why can't I be addicted to prayer?"* St John Cassian answers this question saying that addiction is slavery; you are a slave to what you are addicted to, while prayer is a personal choice to spend time with God. God sent his only begotten Son to give us freedom, not to make us his slaves. Therefore, the decision to stand up and pray is a conscious one, such that we may maintain our free will. That is why Abba Agathon described prayer as "warfare to the last breath"

CHAPTER 01

A SHORT PRAYER FOR ALL CHRISTIANS

I n this chapter, I will explore the first statement of the definition of the Arrow Prayer. I will do so by dividing the chapter into two parts: the first part being the fact that *it is a short prayer* and the second being that *it is prayed by all Christians.*

A Short Prayer

As I mentioned earlier, St Paul's exhortation to pray without ceasing was not a radically new teaching but a realistic practice that was intended for all Christians alike. We will see shortly that it had been practiced in the Old Testament (OT) and continued to be practiced in the New, through the practice of memorizing scripture. You might be wondering *"what's the relationship between memorizing scripture and continuous prayer?"* Though it is true to think that memorizing was for the purpose of reciting the scripture at all times, which we know was practiced by some of the monks, yet reciting long pieces of scripture does not fall under the definition of the Arrow Prayer as being a short prayer.

To understand the relationship between memorization and repeated short prayer, we must look at the ancient practice of memorization. For someone to memorize a large piece of work, one must memorize a number of short formulas that would help him not only memorize the text, but to navigate throughout the text. If he is required, he can start from any point in the text and navigate few lines forward or few lines backward to recite the desired part.

Furthermore, some historians have noticed that the way many ancient writers wrote was influenced by this oral way of thinking which made the text easier to memorize.

Memorising Scripture In The Old Testament:

Intriguingly, education of children in ancient Jewish culture was an integral part of the family life. Studying the Torah was a primary purpose of this system. It was expected that most Jewish children memorise the Torah, or the five books of Moses, by the age of twelve. This came as fulfillment of Gods command to Aaron, "that you may teach the children of Israel all the statutes which the Lord has spoken to them by the hand of Moses" (Leviticus 10:11). Also in the book of Deuteronomy, the Lord explicitly commands the people of Israel, not only the priests but the whole people of Israel, to teach their children His commandments:

> "And these words which I command you today shall be in your heart. You shall teach them diligently to your children, and shall talk of them when you sit in your house, when you walk by the way, when you lie down, and when you rise up. You shall bind them as a sign on your hand, and they shall be as frontlets between your eyes. You shall write them on the doorposts of your house and on your gates." Deuteronomy 6:6

As soon as the child learns the Torah, they fulfill the command above by binding a phylacteries, which is a leather box containing vellum with the Torah written on it, on their head and on their left arm. You can see this practice until today in Jerusalem. Placing it on their forehead is a constant reminder to keep God's law in their memory and the one on their left arm, which is close to the heart, is a reminder to keep and obey God's commandments in the Torah.

It is important to consider this command in its historical context. To a twenty first century reader this sounds like God is asking them for a feat of memory, as we do with Sunday school kids memorising the psalms today. However, this was a culture in which there were no books and if they were available most people could read them and if they could read them, they could not afford to own them. Therefore, the only way the people of God would have access to the word of God, other than hearing it being read once a week in the temple, would be through memorising it.

Memorising Scripture In The Time Of Jesus:

Josephus is one of the Jewish historians who lived in the first century AD. He depicts the Jews of the time as though the primary care of all Jewish parents was the "education of Children" (Against Apion 1:12) in the law of the Lord, according to the commandments in the scripture. Thus, the primary purpose of education in the Jewish context was the learning of, and obedience to the scriptures. The other place where young boys would memorise scripture was in the temple or, if you don't live in Jerusalem, the synagogues.

We also learn from a second century text called "Protevangelium of James," that St Mary was offered to the temple as a young girl. It was allowed for young virgins to live in the temple to fulfil the necessary tasks of the temple such as sewing and creating vestments, washing the vestments of the priests which would be stained regularly by animal blood, preparing liturgical linen, weaving the veil of the Temple, and most importantly, liturgical prayer. There is no clear mention of St Mary or young girls in general to have a school in the temple dedicated to memorising scripture, yet from reading the first chapter of Luke we notice something very interesting.

17

When St Mary met with Elizabeth after she discovered that she was going to be the mother of God, they exchanged a very intimate conversation commonly known as the *Magnificat*. In close study of the prayer of St Mary, we notice a large number of biblical quotations from all over the Old Testament, which indicates that she memorised large portions of the Old Testament by heart.

The Magnificat (Luke 1:46-55)	Old Testament Reference
v47 - My soul magnifies the Lord, And my spirit has rejoiced in God my Saviour	1 Sam 2:1; Is 61:10; Hab 3:18; Ps 25:2 (LXX); 145:6; 28:7
v48 - For He has regarded the lowly state of His maidservant	1 Sam 1:11
V48 - For behold, henceforth all generations will call me blessed	Gen 30:13;
v49 - For He who is mighty has done great things for me, And holy is His name	Ps 103:1; 105:3; 111:9; 145:21
v50 - And His mercy is on those who fear Him From generation to generation	Ps 103:17
v51 - He has shown strength with His arm; He has scattered the proud in the imagination of their hearts	Ps 89:10; 113:7-8
v52 - He has put down the mighty from their thrones, And exalted the lowly	Job 5:11; 12:19; Ps 107:41; 113:7-8; 1 Sam 2:8; Is 40:29
v53 - He has filled the hungry with good things, And the rich He has sent away empty	Ps 107:9; 1 Sam 2:5
v54 - He has helped His servant Israel, In remembrance of His mercy	Is 41:8-9; Ps 98:3
v55 - As He spoke to our fathers, To Abraham and to his seed forever	Gen 12:3; 13:15; 22: 16-18; 26:3-4; 28:13-14; Ps 105:8-10

Memorising Scripture In Late Antiquity:

Memorising scripture remained a common practice in the church as we read in many of the monastic hagiography and literature. In the Pachomian monasteries for example, we know from the rules that no one was accepted into the community unless he knew how to read. If he did not know how, they would spend some time outside the monastery to learn how to read before they joined.

In the rules, he emphatically states: "there shall be no one whatsoever in the monastery who does not learn to read." The requirement to be able to read was so that the new monk was able to read and memorise the scripture.

The Life of St Shenouda narrates how the prophet Jeremiah was weeping over a brother who was reciting the book of Jeremiah, but without heartfelt zeal. While another brother was reciting the book of Ezekiel, Abba Shenouda saw the Prophet Ezekiel appearing to be impressed with his recitation. Another brother was sitting in the corner reciting the twelve prophets. From the text *The History of the Patriarchs,* we know that the monks from St Macarius monastery in the seventh century memorised the psalms by heart in order to recite them during the synaxes.

This was not only the practice of eremitic (communal) monasticism, but it was a practice that some saints practiced from childhood. In the *teaching* of Abba Psote bishop of Psoi, he testifies that in his childhood, "the angel of the Lord has appeared unto me several times while [he] was pasturing [his] father's sheep, and he never ceased to recite the Scripture to me in my abode until I knew them all by heart." St Pisentius also learned by heart twelve books of the scripture while only seven years old.

Memorisation And The Formula:

We are not told in any of these cases the technique these monks used to memoriese, or whether they used formulas. Yet, by studying the school system of the time, we know for certain that using a formula to memorise a long piece of text was a requirement for memory.

By studying the hundreds of school exercises found in ancient rubbish heaps in the desert of Egypt, scholars found a great number of them that had a list of formulas. These had undoubtedly been written for the purpose of the memorisation of a larger text. These lists of formulas were found in secular schools and monastic schools alike. In the excavation of the monasteries such as St Epiphanius, the monastery of St Phoebammon, which was built on the ruins of a pharaonic temple near Epiphanius's monastery, deir el-Gizaz (the glass monastery near Alexandria) and the monastery at Naqlun there are a number of texts of the Coptic alphabet or syllables, which are typical to a school setting. They were found written on ostraca, papyri or parchment. Excavations have also uncovered a large number of lists of formulas from the psalms and other books of the bible.

A recent discovery at the Moharak monastery in modern day Assiut, a fourteenth-century manuscript containing a passage from the teaching of Abba Philemon about the Jesus Prayer was found. What is interesting about this discovery is the fact that, throughout this manuscript, there are various short prayers to Jesus written in the margins that are not a part of the text.

These findings not only indicate that there were a good number of monks from different monasteries around Egypt who were educated, but also that these monks were memorising large texts from the bible. To do so, they had to memorise and continuously repeat all these short formulas on daily basis.

The practice of memorising formulas in order to recollect a large text was not a monastic invention but was broadly used in schools. The person responsible for its innovation was a poet named Simonides in fourth century BC. Once, while he was performing in a function hall in Thessaly, the roof of the hall collapsed minutes after he left the function. In an attempt to identify the bodies of the guests in the function hall he formulated the requirements for a good memory. To be able to remember the order of the guests, he had to denote markers in the hall and form mental images of things he wished to remember. To be able to remember a certain position in the hall, he would refer to the specific marker or anchor that he memorised and navigate the area around this anchor.

Similarly, the way to memorise a long text is to memoriae anchors, which are made up of short formulas. These short formulas would help you recollect the text when you need to. These formulas also allow the mind to skim throughout the text backwards and forwards from the anchor point without having to start from the beginning of the text.

The relationship between building architecture and memorisation is also found in the Old Testament. In chapter 40 of the book of Ezekiel, God commanded him to tell the people of Israel everything he sees in a vision. In the vision, he saw buildings that looked like a city and was commanded to measure the buildings, which contained gates and thresholds. These had a symbolic meaning he was required to tell the people of Israel. Presenting the vision to Ezekiel in an architectural scene made it easier for Ezekiel and his listeners to remember.

An early church writer by the name of Origen also uses buildings, such as the tabernacle, in a metaphorical expression of the constant reminder for the practice of virtue and memorisation of the scripture. In his commentary on the book of Exodus, he interpreted the architecture of the tabernacle as a reminder for memorising the Word of God:

> Let him have an ark of the covenant in which are the tablets of the Law, that "he may *meditate on the Law of God* day and night." (Ps 1: 2) and let his *memory become an ark and library of the books* of God because the prophet also says those are blessed who hold his commands *in memory* that they may do them (Ps 105: 3).

21

The Monastic Cell And Memory

In the monastic tradition, the monks' cell is the place where the monk meets with the Saviour. It was expressed in some monastic writings as "The furnace of Babylon where the three children found the Son of God, and it is like the pillar of cloud where God spoke with Moses." For Abba Paul of Tamma, it was the place where the monk would "reign with God." It is the place where the "glory of God will appear to him inside it."

Many sayings in the writings of the desert fathers talk about the importance of staying in the cell. Abba Moses teaches: "go, sit in your cell, and your cell will teach you everything" for many of the desert fathers, staying in the cell was a way of keeping the monks' mind from any distractions and lose his interior watchfulness. Therefore the cell was a holy space where the monk preformed his spiritual work that consisted of continuous prayer and handiwork and eventually allowed the monk to unite with God.

To help the monk recollect his thoughts while in the cell, archaeologists found a few examples of elaborate wall paintings. These seemingly served as a reminder for the monk of his practice of continuous prayer. The most interesting wall painting is in a cell in the monastery of Abba Jeremiah of Christ enthroned and surrounded by the four living creatures. This too, served the monk living in this cell as a reminder of his practice of the continuous prayer; especially considering that these four living creatures are described in the bible as constantly praying before the throne "'Holy, holy, holy is the Lord God Almighty,' who was, and is, and is to come." Revelation 4:8

Another feature often found in monastic cells are the wall inscriptions. These wall inscriptions are usually short prayers to Jesus or on behalf of other monks in the community. The most intriguing of these inscriptions is found in a monastic cell in Kellia from the seventh to the eighth century. This wall inscription advocates the use of the Jesus prayer against those who object to its use, for the reason of the threat of the separation of the Persons of the Trinity. This inscription as translated below attests to the practice of a primitive formula of the Jesus Prayer utilised by monks in this area. This inscription also points to an earlier controversy that St Shenouda in the fourth century mentioned in one of his sermons, which we will come back to in a later chapter.

But as for us, we know that if we
pray to Jesus, we pray to the
Father and Him, and the Holy Spirit
of the Father with Him again.
For it may not happen that we divide
the divine and holy Trinity,
but rather it is fitting to pray (thus); if we
say 'Christ Jesus', we say
'the Son of God, the Father':
we say 'the Father of Christ, Jesus',
and we complete every prayer with Him;
we say 'through Your only
Son, our Lord Jesus Christ'."

Therefore, these sources gives us a very good reason to believe that the memorisation techniques used in the secular classroom and implemented in the monasteries were responsible for the development of the practice of the Arrow Prayer.

For All Christians

The second part of this statement in the definition of the arrow prayer, describes the prayer as being for all Christians rather than being only for monks and nuns. There are amble references in the sources that clearly endorse this fact. The best way to present these sources is to present them chronologically.

St Shenouda The Archimandrite:

The first of these sources comes from the fourth century from one of the sermons of St Shenouda called, "I am Amazed". We know from the life of St Shenouda that he often gave sermons, not only to the 2200 monks at his white monastery, but lay people from the village were also invited to attend and listen to his sermons.

The circumstances behind this sermon are that a group of Origenist had misinterpreted one of his works by claiming that it is not right that we should pray to Jesus. Rather, they suggested, our prayers should be directed to God the Father since it was to Him Jesus himself prayed. St Shenouda's reply was, "When we say 'Jesus', we speak of the consubstantial Trinity... When we name Jesus we name the Holy Trinity".

He then lists a practical way for his monastic listeners to pray to Jesus, which basically outlines their day to day activities. Following this, he turns his attention to the lay villagers who are listening to his sermon and gives them a similar list:

> Seek after the fulfilment of these words and you will find them on your lips and on the lips of your children.
> When you celebrate a feast and are joyful, (say) 'Jesus.'
> When you are grieving in heart and are distressed, (say) 'Jesus.'
> When your sons and daughters laugh, (say) 'Jesus.'
> The one who draws water, 'Jesus'.
> The one who runs in the face of barbarians, 'Jesus'.
> Those who see wild beasts and something frightening, 'Jesus'.
> Those who are suffering with pains and illnesses, 'Jesus'.
> Those who are taken as prisoners of war, 'Jesus'.
> Those who have suffered perversion of justice and violent treatment, 'Jesus'.
> The name of the one who is on their lips is their salvation and their life, he himself along with the Father

Evidently, for St Shenouda the practice of the continuous prayer is a practice for the monks as much as it is for the lay people and it is supposed to be practiced along with our everyday activities.

Lord Have Mercy:

Liturgical prayers are a perfect example of a bridge that crosses over between laity and monastics, as they both observe at least some prayers simultaneously. When we pay attention to liturgical prayers we find a number of formulas that are frequently repeated; some from the earliest known liturgies such as "Lord have mercy" and "Amen" and are still used until today.

The purpose of the use of repeated formulas in liturgical prayers is to give the participants a formula to meditate on during the day for the purpose of memorising the song.

The *"Kyrie Eleison"* or the *"Lord have mercy"* formula was first used in liturgical prayer and is evident in the liturgy of St Basil which contains numerous responses of the *"Lord have mercy."* Other than St Basil's liturgy, it is attested to in the 14th century account of the Coptic historian Youhanna Ibn Zakaria, whereby in the rite of Good Friday, after praying the four Gospels of the 12th hour, the priests and congregation say *"Kyrie Eleison"* 400 times - 100 times facing each direction prostrating each with each recitation. This rite continues to be practised in the church to this day.

An earlier incident that seems to have affected the frequent repetition of the prayer with prostrations is recorded in the *History of the Patriarchs*. When the 'Muizz' (969 – 979AD) wanted to test the Christian faith through the instigation of the Jewish minister, he asked the Patriarch to fulfil the Bible verse, "if you have faith the size of a mustard seed you will say to this mountain, 'Move from here to there,' and it will move" (Mt 17: 20). As instructed by the Virgin Mary, the Patriarch brought Simon the tanner who asked the Patriarch:

"Go out with your priests and all your people to the mountain concerning which the king told you, (having) with you gospels, crosses, censers and large candles. Let the king stand with his soldiers and his troops on one side, and you and your people, on one side, and I, behind you, will stand in the midst of the people, so that no one may recognize me. Then read you and your priests and cry aloud, saying: 'O Lord, have mercy' for a long time. Then command them to be silent and (to keep) quiet, and you shall prostrate yourself and all who are with you shall prostrate themselves, and I will prostrate myself with you such that no one recognizes me. Do thus three times, and every time that you shall prostrate yourself and stand up (again) you shall make (the sign of) the cross over the mountain, and you shall see the glory of God'."

On a personal level, this short prayer was also used and recommended by monks as in the account of Abba Philemon which records that he "repeated within 'Lord have mercy' with his whole attention and for a considerable time."

The Psalis:

Another liturgical prayer that makes use of repeated formulas is the Psali, which is believed to be written during the seventh to the ninth centuries. The earliest manuscript tradition for this prayer comes from the twelfth or thirteenth century, and the earliest complete manuscript of the Psalis comes from the fourteenth century in the writings of Abu Al-Barakat The Psalis are simply praises for Jesus Christ and each stanza ends with a repeated formula that praises the name of Jesus. This Psalis are used in Coptic Church until today in monasteries and parish churches alike.

The Book Of The Master And Disciple:

The eleventh and twelfth centuries saw a great decline in the use of the Coptic language among the Copts while the liturgical books where not yet translated to the Arabic language. We know this from a church canon, which comes from patriarch Gabriel Ibn Turayk, the 70th Patriarch of Alexandria (1131-1145). This canon instruct bishops to:

> "instruct the Christian people whom he pastors, and to teach them by heart the *Doxa*, the Prayer which the Lord Christ taught his disciples, and the holy Creed, *in the language that they know and understand,* in order thus to pray during times of prayer, and *not* to jabber senselessly *[yahd'i]* in what they do not know

Moreover, the eleventh century text, *The Master and Disciple,* recounts questions and answers by an anonymous master and a disciple about different aspects of the Christian life. One of the questions asked by the disciple is: "What is the ascription of praise and holiness *[al-tasbih wal-taqdis]* that is obligatory for the believer?" The master answers:

> The early morning prayer when he arises from sleep, before all work. Let him pray to the best of his ability and say in his prayer whatever [prayers] he might know; but it will suffice him that he say:
>
> > "My Lord Jesus, have mercy on me!
> > My Lord Jesus, help me!
> > I praise you, my Lord Jesus, and bow down to you!"

These three words will suffice him if he does not know anything besides them.

It is very clear that this text was not intended for a monastic audience, on the contrary, the text continues:

> "Whether man or woman; let them pray it before their labour for their subsistence.
>
> a) At sunset, let him pray and prostrate himself as in the early morning prayer.
> b) The bedtime prayer, before he goes to sleep. Let him pray and prostrate himself as in the early morning and the evening prayers.
>
> These three [prayers] are incumbent upon [each] man and woman every day; they have no pretext before God for neglecting them. As for the other four, it is incumbent upon them to pray them while in their places of livelihood, whether seated or standing, riding or walking, with their faces directed wherever they were, because the Lord is in every place and every direction.

He then concludes:

> Other than that, let the name of the Lord Jesus be always in their hearts and mouths. Whenever one thinks of him, let one say:
> "My Lord Jesus, have mercy on me!
> My Lord Jesus, help me!
> I praise you, my Lord Jesus!

Therefore, it seems that due to the lack of Arabic translations of the Agpia, the church prescribed the Arrow Prayer as an alternative practice until an established Arabic translation of the prayer of the hours was made available.

The writer of this text directly instructed the lay people to pray without ceasing and, in a similar manner, St Shenouda lists the different daily activities that the prayer should accompany.

St Bulus Al Bushi

St Bulus al Bushi (1170-1250) was the first bishop of Cairo after the city was made the official capital of Egypt. He was also one of the first Christian writers in the Arabic language. He has a number of writings, some of which include his eight homilies on the feasts of the Lord. In the homily for the feast of Annunciation he asked his listeners, who were from the laity, to constantly remember the name of the Lord:

> "So now let reading the inspired books be your pride as well as singing God's words, your honour is in standing up in prayer, your consolation is your constant joy in the Lord, your hope is in your relentless communication with Him, Remembrance of His holy name be your food, as David has said: if I remember you, my soul is satisfied as from marrow and fatness. (Psalm 63:5)

Thus in retrospect, in contrast to the assumption we have today of the practice of continuous prayer as being exclusive to monks and clergy, the use of the arrow prayer was clearly seen throughout the history of the church as a prayer practiced by both laity and monastics alike. While there are many gaps in history where we don't have any reference to the practice of the arrow prayer, we know definitively that it was practiced in liturgical prayers, which ultimately kept the practice of the prayer alive.

CHAPTER
02

THE LANGUAGE OF THE SCRIPTURE

W hen we read the writing of the early church fathers we find a great number of biblical quotations and allusion. To the extent that many scholars agree that we can reconstruct the whole bible only from the quotations of the bible found in the writings of the church fathers. To better understand the background from which this came to occur, we need to understand the meaning of one of the Greek words that we often read in the bible, as well as in the writing of the church fathers.

The Meaning Of *Meléte* Or To Meditate:

When we come across the verb to meditate, we usually assume it to mean to *contemplate*. We picture it as someone looking into the horizon or sunrise in deep musing about the meaning of life. This is not what the word meant in the Greek language. The meaning of the word *Meléte* came from its use in the Greek philosophical school which had the connotation of studying in a meditative manner. Defined otherwise, and more practically, it was the practice of the repetition of phrases for the purpose of interiorizing the message that the phrase is teaching (the equivalent Arabic word is *Hazeez*).

Meditation In The Old Testament:

To give one vivid example of meditation in the Old Testament, we need to read psalm 118 (119), which is the longest psalm in the bible. We also pray this psalm in the Coptic tradition every night in the first service of the midnight prayer of the Agpia.

Psalm 118 (119) is made up of twenty-two paragraphs, with each paragraph beginning with a letter from the Hebrew alphabet. Every paragraph has 8 verses that start with the same letter of the alphabet, which means the whole psalm is made up of 176 verses. This is very common practice in oral culture to help the poet remember the poetry and be able to recite it. Furthermore, it enables the listeners to memorise it for their own use.

The theme that runs through the psalms is David's love for the Word of God and how he meditates on His word day and night. In this psalm, he uses nine different synonyms for the word of God (Law, Precepts, Testimonies, Way, Statutes, Commandment, Judgments, Word, and Truth). By meditating on the word of God as the psalm indicates, the psalmist and those who use the psalm are exhorted to pray the Arrow Prayer day and night.

It makes me ashamed of myself knowing how much David was in love with the word of God. Even more so when I consider that at the time of David, there were only the five books of Moses. These included Leviticus, Deuteronomy and Numbers (the exact three books I skip when reading the Bible).

The monks of Egypt particularly used this psalm as they saw the Word of God as Jesus Himself. You can even read the whole psalm replacing any of these synonyms with the word "Jesus". Which makes the whole psalm a daily prayer to Jesus. There is some evidence that reveals the way the monks of Egypt have adapted the psalm to be a devotion to Jesus.

When you read paragraph 13.1 from the bible which reads "O how I love your law" and you read the same paragraph from the book of the Agpia you find it was changed to say "O how I love your name" The other modification you will find in the refrain which reads, "Glory be to you O lover of Mankind," which is a praise to Jesus normally sung after every paragraph.

Meditation In The Desert:

For a long time scholars have assumed that the early monks were mostly uneducated. Recent studies show that not only was there a good number of educated monks in the desert, but that there were class rooms to educate monks who have not been to school before joining the monastery. As mentioned previously, there was even a condition for joining the monastery in the Pachomian monastic rules.

By being educated, the monks were familiar with teaching techniques and methods of the secular school of the time. One of these methods was the practice of meditation. In fact, the three steps of secular education in antiquity was as follows. The first step is to learn a new concept, then you meditate (*Melété*) on this concept by repeating throughout the day to interiorize the concept, then finally to put this concept into practice. These three steps nicely aligned with the practice of meditation in a monastic setting.

Meditation was always listed as one of the monastic ascetic practices required by monks along with prayer and fasting. Abba Lot described his discipline to Abba Joseph, saying "I say my little office, I fast a little, I pray and meditate". Another elder lists the foundations of the monastic life to be "meditation, psalmody, and manual work". It is also said of Abba John the Dwarf that, after he returned from harvest, "he gave himself to prayer, meditation and psalmody until his thoughts were re-established in their previous order". St Macarius advised a monk who was attacked by thoughts, saying: "Practice fasting a little later; meditate on the Gospel and the other Scriptures". An anonymous elder said that the life of a monk consists of "obedience, meditation, not judging, not slandering, not complaining". Another anonymous elder said that the key to fighting against the devil is to "Practise silence, be careful for nothing, give heed to your meditation, lie down and get up in the fear of God, and you will not need to fear the assaults of the impious". Abba Poemen described sitting in one's cell as consisting of "manual work, eating only once a day, silence and meditation".

The topic of meditation usually involved verses from the bible or a word of the elder. In the *AP*, when Abba Betimes and Abba Ammonas visited Abba Achilles, they "heard him meditating this phrase: fear not Joseph to go down to Egypt [Gen 46:3]; and he went on meditating this phrase for a long time". The same Abba Amoi, after kicking Abba John the short out of his cell to test his patience, came to Abba John's cell and found him audibly repeating verses from the scriptures that would calm his soul against Abba John's harsh treatment: "endure every lesson, 'for what son does not have his father instruct him?'" [Heb 12:7] And again, "by your endurance you will gain your souls" [Matt 24:13; Luke 21:19], and again, "The one who endures to the end will be saved" [Matt 24:13]"

Furthermore, the connection between meditation on verses of the scripture and praying unceasing prayers can be demonstrated in the teachings of Abba Amoi's to St John the short. Abba Amoi said that, while walking to church which was a far distance from where he lived, "to meditating on the scriptures inspired by God, ruminating on them in his heart with unceasing prayer [1 Thess 5:17] like a spiritual sheep, drawing the spirit to him through the sweetness of their meaning" .

Consuming The Word Of God:

The concept of digesting and interiorising the repeated text of the scriptures was such a common practice in the desert, that it was used as a metaphor for continuous prayer. The metaphor for eating and digesting the word was first used in the bible in Ezekiel 3:3, Revelation 10: 9-10 and Psalm 33:9 where the word of God was given to the prophet to eat and that it was sweet in his mouth.

Again, it is important to make the point that the concept of meditation and interiorising the text was not unique to the monastic fathers but also an important practice by secular philosophers and educators. It is important to make this point to emphasise the fact that the practice of the Arrow Prayer was as common to monastics and non-monastics alike. Quintilian, one of the first century educators wrote:

> We do not swallow our food till we have chewed it and reduced it almost to a state of liquefaction to assist the process of digestion, so what we read must not be committed to the memory for subsequent imitation while it is still in a crude state, but must be softened and, if I may use the phrase, reduced to a pulp by frequent re-perusal.

In Origin's commentary of the book of Leviticus he interprets the verse "Chew the cud and part the hoof" (Lev. 11:4) using the same metaphor. The one who chews the cud is the one who "pays heed to knowledge and 'meditates day and night on the law of the Lord'". Philo, the first century Jewish philosopher and interpreter of the Old Testament from Alexandria, in his contemplation of the same verse interprets "chewing the cud" to mean meditating on what one has learned; "dividing the hoof" means separating good aspects of memory from evil

In the monastic literature, St Macarius elaborately describes a childhood experience and relates it to the word of God:

> I know that when I was a child I used to observe that the old women and the young people were chewing something in their mouths so that it would sweeten the saliva in their throats and the bad breath of their mouths, sweetening and refreshing their liver and all their innards. If something

35

fleshly can so sweeten those who chew it and ruminate it, then how much more the food of life, the spring of salvation, the fount of living water, the sweet of all sweets, our Lord Jesus Christ! If the demons hear his glorious name blessed by our mouths, they vanish like smoke. This blessed name, if we persevere in it and ruminate on it, opens up the spirit, the charioteer of the soul and the body and drives all thoughts of evil out of the immortal soul and reveals to it heavenly things

Breathing The Word Of God

Another metaphor that has been used for meditating is breathing. This metaphor was not initially as prevalent as the eating metaphor, yet during the fourteenth century it gained more popularity especially after the monks of Mount Athos added the practice of stillness and breathing techniques while praying the Jesus prayer.

In the *Life of St Anthony*, when he was exhorting his disciple before his death not to be fearful of the plots of the demons, "but instead draw inspiration [lit. breath in] from Christ and believe in him." "Breathing in" Christ is an expression borrowed from the philosophical school. Similarly, St Theodore the disciple of St Pachomius, refers to the scripture as being the breath of God

St John Climacus, makes a better connection between the practice of meditating on short verses and breathing in more than one of this sayings:

> "Take in with your very breath the word of Him who said:
> "he that endureth to the end shall be saved"
> "Let this cleave to your breathing, the word of him who says: 'But as for me, when demons trouble me, I put on sackcloth, and humbled my soul with fasting, and my prayer hath cleaved to the bosom of my soul'"
> "Let the remembrance of Jesus be present with each breath, and then you will know the value of stillness"

36

It is very important to consider St John Climacus when we talk about breathing as a metaphor, as he is often quoted when arguing in favor of using special breathing techniques while practicing the Jesus prayer as the prayer developed in the fourteenth century at Mount Athos. Yet, it is important to know that the saint used it as a metaphor rather than describing an old practice. In one of the eighth century texts relating to St Macarius, who has already used eating as a metaphor, he also uses breathing as a metaphor: "It is not easy to say with each breath Lord Jesus have mercy on me, I bless you my Lord Jesus"

This is consistent with the ancient understanding of breathing biologically, which was thought that the breath goes from the lungs to the heart and the heart was often understood as being the center of the human being. Therefore, repeating the words or phrases in meditation for the purpose of interiorizing them meant to keep them in the persons core (their heart).

The Language Of The Scripture

Now that we learned what meditation means and how people throughout history have meditated, it is important to know the extent to which they used scripture for meditation. As I mentioned before, there is a strong link between memorisation and meditation. Since, to memorise a passage or a long text, one must constantly repeat or meditate on a number of formulas throughout the text to make the memorising possible. We have amble evidence from monastic writings that suggest that memorising scripture was an integral part in the life of the monk. Henceforth, it would be appropriate to conclude that the Bible was the primary source of inspiration for the Arrow Prayer formula.

Biblical Literacy

During the nineteenth and early twentieth centuries, it was believed by many scholars that the early monks had a poor knowledge of the scripture. They explained some of the references found in the monastic writings as nothing more than superficial accomplishment that did not penetrate the heart but rather, it was their way of adding a biblical tinge to their teachings. This opinion was highly influenced by the views of the early protestant reformers such as Wycliffe and Luther, as a response to their resentment to monasticism in Europe at the time.

Recent scholarship has found a radically different understanding of early monasticism and its interaction with the bible. As Burton-Christie affirms, "the growing consensus on this issue suggests that primitive monasticism cannot adequately be understood apart from the consideration of the place of scripture in its formation and ongoing life"

In the *sayings*, we encounter obvious oppositions towards owning bible books: "A brother said to Abba Serapion, 'Give me a word.' The old man said to him, 'What shall I say to you? You have taken the living of the widows and orphans and put it on your shelves.' For he saw them full of books" and St Macarius advised Abba Theodore of Pherme, to sell the bible books he acquired for the benefit of the monks:

> Abba Theodore of Pherme had acquired three good books. He came to Abba Macarius and said to him, "I have three good books from which I derive profit; the brethren also make use of them and derive profit from them. Tell me what I ought to do: keep them for my use and that of the brethren, or sell them and give the money to the poor?" The old man answered him in this way, "your actions are good; but it is best for all to possess nothing." Hearing that, he went and sold his books and gave the money for them to the poor

It is clear then, that the opposition of the desert fathers was not towards the bible itself, as we read many other sayings that emphasised the use of scripture. Abba Epiphanius, bishop of Cyprus was emphatic about this point:

"The acquisition of Christian books is necessary for those who can use them. For the mere sight of these books renders us less inclined to sin, and incites us to believe more firmly in righteousness."

"He also said, 'Reading the Scriptures is a great safeguard against sin.'"

"He also said, 'It is a great treachery to salvation to know nothing of the divine law.'"
"He also said, 'Ignorance of the Scriptures is a precipice and a deep abyss.'"

However the opposition was towards owning a bible. Owning a book that size in antiquity was a valuable possession that did not suit a monk who vowed poverty. Yet we know that the Monasteries of St Shenouda and St Pachomius had an extensive library with a large number of books. In fact, there were special rules to regulate the borrowing of books. These books were not owned by any one of the monks but it was in the monastery's common library, therefore it did not contradict the vow of poverty.

Another reason that accounts for the apparent hostility towards owning a bible book was not necessary a call to poverty. Rather, in oral culture, having the words written down in a book rather than memorising them can leads the monk to neglect his practice of continuous prayer - which was a part of the memorizing process. We know from the *Life* of St Anthony that, "He prayed all the time, having learned that it is necessary to pray without ceasing. Indeed he paid such close attention to what was read in Church that nothing in the Scriptures escaped his notice. He kept everything in his heart, with the result that in his heart, memory took the place of books"

Moreover, it runs the risk of stripping the spoken word of its power. The spoken word gave the listener the urgency to do the word rather than put it on the shelf. An elder in the anonymous collection of the sayings expressed this negative progression. He said, "The prophets wrote books, then came our fathers who put them into practice. Those who came after them learned them by heart, then came the present generation, who have written them out and put them into their window seats without using them" We see similar battle today between printed and electronic books.

The Bible In Monastic Writings

One of the main features of monastic writings is that they are inundated with biblical references. Armand Veilleux's translation of the Coptic and Greek lives of St Pachomius, the rules of Horisius and Theodore his successors, gives sixty pages of biblical references from all over the bible. In addition to the other translations of the lives of saints that more often than not contain references from every book of the bible.

The Rules of St Pachomius makes it clear that "there shall be no one whatsoever in the monastery who does not learn to read and does not memorise something of the scripture. [One should learn by heart] at least the New Testament and the Psalter" In terms of reciting the bible, it was made clear in the rules that it should be practiced at all times: "When the *synaxis* is dismissed, each one shall recite something from the scripture while going either to his cell or to the refectory"

In the *Life* of St Shenouda, as mentioned in the previous chapter, three particular anecdotes stand out. The prophet Jeremiah was seen by the saint weeping over a brother who was reciting the book of Jeremiah without heartfelt ardour Another brother was praised by the prophet Ezekiel because "his recitation," said the prophet, "truly strikes home" Abba Shenoute saw another brother who was sitting in the corner reciting the twelve Minor Prophets

St Anthony expected his monks to know the scriptures very well that he instructed one of the brothers: "whatever you do, do it according to the testimony of the holy scripture"

The translation of the AP has caused disagreement among scholars about the number of biblical quotations in the text. The number of quotations varies from 93 to 485 biblical references in the same text. The root of the disagreement stems from the criteria that different scholars used to identify a reference. This varied from a direct biblical quote which was often introduced with the phrases "as it is written" as in this example:

> The old man [abba Moses] was asked, 'What is the good of the fasts and watchings which a man imposes on himself?' and he replied, 'They make the soul humble. For it is written, "Consider my affliction and my trouble, and forgive all my sins." (Ps.25.18)

Or referring to a specific bible character or story without a direct quote as in this example:

> With regard to receiving the brethren, the same abba [Apollo] said that one should bow before the brethren who come, because it is not before them, but before God that we prostrate ourselves. 'When you see your brother,' he said, 'you see the Lord your God.' He added, 'We have learnt that from Abraham. (cf. Gen. 18) When you receive the brethren, invite them to rest awhile, for this is what we learn from Lot who invited the angels to do so.' (cf. Gen. 19.3)

An allusion to a biblical reference was also utilised on occasion:

> A brother asked Abba Poemen, 'What shall I do, for fornication and anger war against me?' The old man said, 'In this connection David said: "I will pierce the lion and I will slay the bear" (cf 1 Sam. 17.35); that is to say: I will cut off anger and I will crush fornication with hard labour.'

The scriptural allusion in this saying goes deeper than quoting the bible verse as the two animals were not randomly chosen. The lion, which symbolises violent anger, has been referred to many times in the bible and the bear, being the desire of the flesh, is used by Hesychius in his commentary to Amos 5:19.

Another criteria is the explanation of a bible verse to illustrate a virtue. In this case it is about judging others:

> Abba Poemen said, it is written: "Give witness of that which your eyes have seen" (Proverbs 25.8); but I say to you even if you have touched with your hands, do not give witness. In truth, a brother was deceived in this respect; he thought he saw his brother in the act of sinning with a woman; greatly incensed, he drew near and kicked them (for he thought it was they), saying, "Now stop; how much longer will you go on?" Now it turned out that it was some sheaves of corn. That is the reason why I said to you: even if you touch with your hands, do not reprove"

In this saying, Abba Poemen explains a bible verse about judging others and he illustrates his teaching with a story. What is intriguing about the saying is how it ends. Abba Poemen finishes the saying with a teaching that goes beyond the bible verse. He initially uses the bible verse then he personalised it to make his point regarding judging others, "even if you touch with your hands," to emphasise his teaching. We find many examples of the desert fathers using the verses of the bible as their own depending on the situation, while keeping true to the meaning of the verse.

Some of the sayings do not necessary quote the bible at all, but the layout of the saying matches some biblical stories. In the case below, the saying mimics Jesus interaction with the rich young man in Matt 19:16-22. While they do not quote exact biblical phrases, the structure and language of the sayings directly matches the biblical account.

> A brother questioned an old man saying, 'What good work

should I do so that I may live?' The old man said, 'God knows what is good. I have heard it said that one of the Fathers asked Abba Nisterus the Great, the friend of Abba Anthony, and said to him, "What good work is there that I could do?" He said to him, "Are not all actions equal? Scripture says that Abraham was hospitable and God was with him. David was humble, and God was with him. Elias loved interior peace and God was with him. So, do whatever you see your soul desires according to God and guard your heart."

These different ways in which the desert fathers used the scripture in their everyday speech, makes scholars' lives hard trying to untangle the words of the elder from those of the scripture. Additionally, it illustrates the way scripture was mingled with the desert fathers' everyday speech. It is often difficult to work out where the word of the *Abba* stops and the scripture begins. They were not trying to explain the scripture, nor did they merely quote it, but their everyday language was the language of the scripture.

When we further read other monastic and patristic writings, we see a very common style of quoting scripture. This is achieved by writing paragraphs, which are made up of strings of biblical verses from throughout the bible. St Athanasius, for example, in one of his writings, *Against the Arians*, uses strings of bible verses from Deuteronomy, Psalms, Isaiah, John, Matthew, Philemon, and 1 Corinthians to paraphrase St Peter's Pentecostal speech, in order to explain a troublesome phrase in Act 2:36. St Pachomius also uses the same style in his rules to convey a specific point. From our time we only need to read few pages from any of the library of writings of Pope Shenouda III to see this style of writings being employed.

Outside the monastery, we know St Augustine and many other Alexandrian fathers used a number of half verses and key phrases from all over the bible in their sermons to allow the listeners to recall biblical stories and teachings as he makes his point. This also allows for listeners to memorise the sermon. Anyone who grew up listening to the sermons of Pope Shenouda would have a large library of bible verses committed to memory from his constant repetition of biblical verses in his sermons.

This was not a literary technique, but the result of the daily exercise of memorising and meditating on the scripture. The practice of *Melétē* in order to memorise the bible formed their everyday speech and action, which in turn highlights the pervasiveness of the practice of continuous prayer, using short verses from the bible among the monks of Egypt.

Talking Back:

One of the most prolific monastic writers in the Egyptian desert during the fourth century is a monk named Evagrius. His writings on different ascetical practices have been an invaluable expression of the monastic ascetic practices of the fourth century. One of his writings titles *Antirrhetikos* or "Talking Back," is made up of a list of nearly five hundred thoughts that can afflict a monk followed by short biblical verses that a monk should repeat in his mind to fight against these thoughts. For example, if a monk has thoughts that remind him of past feasting and drinking he should say, "it is better to go into the house of mourning than to go into the house of drinking" (Ecclesiastes 7:2). Against a thought of gluttony on feast days and the memory of feasting at the finest table he should say: "But I will exult in the Lord and rejoice in my savior" (Heb 3:18). Against a thought of anger towards your brother due to his laziness you say: "if you are angry with a brother, you will be liable to judgment" (Matt 5:22).

The idea of answering back demonic thoughts with biblical verses is very biblical for Evagrius. In the prologue to *Talking Back,* he points to Jesus' use of biblical verses when he was tempted on the mountain after spending forty days in prayer and fasting: "Our Lord Jesus Christ… handed on to us what he himself did when he was tempted by Satan. In the time of struggle, when the demons make war against us and hurl their arrows at us, let us answer them from the holy scriptures."

The Bible In Hagiography

It is important to consider how different saints used the bible or short prayers such as the Jesus prayer in their continuous prayer. It is particularly important to consider those saints who are not monks or bishop to illustrate the widespread use of the arrow prayer outside of the monastic circles. It is also important to consider these accounts of the lives of saint as they come from different centuries to appreciate its consistent devotion throughout history.

Jirjis Al Muzahim -

Jirjis (George) surnamed Muzahim, is a tenth century martyr who was born to a Muslim father and a Christian mother. As a child, he went to church with his mother and yearned to partake of the holy bread like the other children. When he grew older he was baptized and married a Christian girl. When the authorities knew of his conversion, they tortured him until he was finally martyred. The account of his life and martyrdom is full of references to him repeating the name of Jesus. It is said that "The devil could not bear it seeing him praying to our Lord Jesus Christ day and night and he would not cease from his remembrance." This was his prayer even during his torture: "But as for those who struck him with canes, they did not cease from striking him, but as for the saint, he did not mention anything other than the name of Jesus Christ."

St Barsoum The Naked –

St Barsoum was an ascetic who was not a priest or a monk, yet his *Life* reports numerous details that highlighted his practice of continuous prayer using short verses from the bible.
As a young boy he memorized the bible as the *Life* reports that his

parents "brought him up in all righteousness and learned writing and memorised the Holy Books which is the breath of God" As he grew older he lived the ascetic life outside the city for five years practicing "Continuous prayer without ceasing". When he went to live in St Marcurius' church, on his way he "prayed the psalms till he reached the church" His *Life* frequently reports that he prayed "day and night". This reference to praying at all times follows through to his deathbed when it is mentioned he would "recite the psalms saying "the Lord is my light and my salvation whom shall I fear" and he said: "How pleasant and joyful for the brethren to dwell together" then he made the sign of the holy cross and gave up his spirit."

CHAPTER 03

WORK AND PRAYER – FRIENDS OR FOES?

The third statement from the definition of the Arrow prayer - repeated throughout the day while practicing your day-to-day activities – is probably the most difficult one to apply, yet it is the most practical. It is the most difficult because to pray while doing a physical activity is one thing, but to keep your mind focused while doing an office job or a job that requires mental activity is another. Before we get into that let us see what the fathers said about work and prayer.

Work And Prayer In The Bible:

As we discussed in the last chapter, meditation is the practice of repeating the words of scripture for the purpose of interiorizing them. There is no better place to go to when we speak about meditation than Psalm one. In Psalm one, the psalmist ascribes blessings on the man who meditates on the law of the Lord, day and night. Let's unpack this together. First, the psalmist is not addressing a specific category of people, such as the priests or the Levites but he is addressing all readers of the psalm. This is also evident in the categories of people that this man interacts with on daily basis, the ungodly, the sinners and the scornful. An environment that we all involuntarily find ourselves in throughout our working day.

Second, this man who, despite being in this environment, still finds the time to meditate on the law of the Lord. The psalmist urges the blessed man not only to withdraw from this environment but to further meditate on the law of the Lord day and night. The expression day and night here is not a figure of speech, but a direct order to be in God's presence throughout the day by the practice of meditation, or the constant repetition of memorised prayers throughout the day. As a result of this practice, this man will be like "a tree that brings forth fruit in its season" Psalm 1:3.

In the first chapter of the book of Joshua, God commissions Joshua to complete the great work that Moses started, to take half a million people into the Promised Land. As you can imagine, it is a most challenging task in the life of Joshua or anyone in such a leadership position for that matter. Other than Gods commandment "to be strong and of good courage" (Joshua 1:9), God commands Joshua to make meditation on the word of God his first priority: "This Book of the Law shall not depart from your mouth, but you shall meditate in it day and night, that you may observe to do according to all that is written in it" (Joshua 1: 8). God's command was not as we imagine to study the land, send spies to your enemies or think of a strategic plan to gain the trust of your people. Rather, it was simply to meditate on the law of the Lord and to do according to what is written.

It is important to note here that Joshua was not a single man or a monk, but he was a married man with children. In addition to this, it is also crucial to note that God gave Joshua this commandment not before he goes into the desert for a retreat, but before he went to lead half a million people into the promised land.

Work And Prayer In Monasticism:

In monasticism, work and prayer are the fundamental activity of the monk. This was a lesson St Anthony learned early in his monastic life. When he was once afflicted with depression, an angel appeared to him and showed him the way a monk should live in a vision. He saw an angel in the form of a man "sitting at his work, getting up from his work to pray, then sitting down and plaiting a rope, then getting up again to pray" Not much later, St Pachomius was instructed by Abba Palamon to live the monastic life this way: "vigils from evening to morning in prayers, recitations, and numerous manual labours" St Pachomius passed on to his disciple Theodore, that the work of the monk is "unceasing prayer, vigils, reciting of God's law, and our manual labour" St Macarius lists the work of the monk to "... demonstrate a love of God and a love of people... with manual works, with vigils, with numerous prayers" Not much later, St John Cassian expresses his admiration towards the way the monks of Egypt practice work and prayer:

> "It is hardly possible to determine what depends on what here – that is, whether they practice manual labour ceaselessly thanks to their spiritual meditation or whether they acquired such remarkable progress in the spirit and such luminous knowledge thanks to their constant labour".

The balance between doing manual labour and praying was imperative for the desert monks, to the extent that the temptation to disturb this balance was always met with strict opposition. When one of the brothers in the monastery of St Pachomius was overenthusiastic about doing his handiwork, finishing two mats a day instead of one, the saint chastised his behavior in front of the other monks:

"See this brother; from morning till now he has given all his toil to the devil and has left nothing whatever of his work for the comfort of his own soul, because he has preferred the praise of men to the praise of God. And although he has worn out his body through labour he has made his soul empty of the fruition of the works"

On the other extreme, we have monks who were overenthusiastic about their prayer at the expense of their work. St John the short when he first went to the desert with his brother, he decided to live like angels and go into the desert to live the life of continuous prayer. Being exhausted only a week later, he came knocking on the door of his brother to give him some bread and water, but his brother replied sarcastically: "John no longer lives with human beings, he has become an angel!" and so left him outside all night. In the morning, the brother opened the door and teaching him a lesson told him "You are a human being. To eat you must work"

A similar story is told about Abba Silvanus who wanted to teach a visiting brother who was wanting to spend his time in prayer without doing his handiwork, quoting the bible verses: "Do not labour for the food which perishes" (John 6.27) "Mary has chosen the good portion" (Luke 10.42). When the visiting brother protested after Abba Silvanus intentionally ignored to call him for the meals, Abba Silvanus said to him: "Because you are a spiritual man and do not need that kind of food. We, being carnal, want to eat, and that is why we work. But you have chosen the good portion and read the whole day long and you do not want to eat carnal food"

Work And Prayer Outside The Monastery:

We expect the church to be somewhat lenient on lay people when it comes to ceaseless prayer, yet from our sources we know it was not the case at all. In the same sermon by St Shenouda where he commanded the monks to pray while doing their daily activities, he also spoke to the laypeople in the village who were also listening and commanded them to pray while doing their daily activities:

"Seek after the fulfilment of these words and you will find them on your lips and on the lips of your children.
When you celebrate a feast and are joyful, (say) 'Jesus.'
When you are grieving in heart and are distressed, (say) 'Jesus.'
When your sons and daughters laugh, (say) 'Jesus.'
The one who draws water, 'Jesus'.
The one who runs in the face of barbarians, 'Jesus'.
Those who see wild beasts and something frightening, 'Jesus'.
Those who are suffering with pains and illnesses, 'Jesus'.
Those who are taken as prisoners of war, 'Jesus'.
Those who have severed perversion of justice and violent treatment, 'Jesus'."
The name of the one who is on their lips is their salvation and their life, he himself along with the Father

I can't help but imagine that if St Shenouda was giving the sermon today he would be saying:

When you find a job or get a promotion, say 'Jesus'
When you are depressed or anxious, say 'Jesus'
When you are on the bus or train, say 'Jesus'
When are studying for you children or taking them to school, say 'Jesus'
When you are in the gym or jogging, say 'Jesus'
When you are traveling or visiting family, say 'Jesus'

The idea behind the elaborate list of daily activities is to say that there is no specific time for prayer, but that it permeates our daily activities.

Whenever I visit Egypt I insist on making every effort to visit Old Cairo. This area of Cairo was, for centuries, the center where most people lived and you cannot help but notice how close the churches are from each other. You could spend one or two full days walking around visiting the different churches learning about their individual history and architecture. For anyone living anywhere in the area, you would have at least a church if not more within walking distance from your house. Furthermore, it was a common practice for churches to pray the Agpia prayers together with the congregation before and after work hours. I cannot help but imagine this area as one big monastery where lay people go to church early in the morning on their way to work and on their way back they stop for evening prayers. This is exactly how the monks lived, and still live, in the monastery.

Silent (Nonverbal) Prayers

On a more practical note, there are other ways of prayer that we can practice while we are at work no matter how busy we can get. Studies show that 70-90% of our everyday communication is nonverbal. The same can be said about prayer. We often limit what we call prayer to standing in front of an icon or in church and talking to God. This is an important mode of prayer but by no means the only effective one. We have many biblical examples of these different modes, whose importance I would like to explore. Hanna, the mother of Samuel the Prophet, went to the temple to pray to the Lord for a son. When Eli the priest found her in the temple, "her lips were moving but hearing no sound" (1 Samuel 1:13). This was one of the most effective prayers. As a result of this prayer she gave birth to Samuel the first prophet in the Old Testament.

Today, whilst being on a long drive or commuting to work, we have the opportunity to lift our hearts to God in silent prayers. Before joining the monastery, my confession father always advised me to use the drive to the monastery, which usually took two hours, to talk to God. If I have no one with me in the car, I can speak my prayers out loud, otherwise it can be done silently.

Abba Barsanuphius, one of the desert fathers was once asked about how to practically fulfil the command to pray unceasingly, particularly when you are in the market or among people. To this he replied: "When one is alone, one should recite the psalms and pray with one's mouth and one's heart. However, when one is in the market place or with other people, it is not necessary to recite the psalms with one's mouth, but only with one's mind".

Regarding the sinful woman who washed the feet of Jesus and wiped them with the hair of her head, the gospel writers didn't mention that she said a word to Jesus. She walked in a room of people who looked down at her and would have loved to kick her out of the house if they got the chance. Nevertheless, she ran to Jesus' feet ignoring all the pressure around her.

This is a great example of service for many people who work in the health care and aged care field. Every time you are helping a person in need you should see this person as Jesus Himself. It is very hard sometimes to do this especially when you are, like the sinful woman, surrounded by people who don't share the same motives for doing your job. Jesus Himself promised that "when you did it to one of the least of these my brothers and sisters, you were doing it to me!' (Matthew 25: 40). Therefore, looking at your work from the right lens, your day to day activity at work becomes a silent prayer to God.

Nehemiah in the Old Testament is an excellent example of someone who worked in a highly intense environment, yet he managed to incorporate silent prayers in his daily job. In chapter one of the book of Nehemiah, he prays a long prayer to God about the state of the people of Israel. In his prayer he exclaimed: "Look down and see me praying night and day for your people Israel" (Nehemiah 1: 6). This was not a figure of speech as you would expect.

When he went to work the next day, his face was sad in front of the king. Before I go on, he worked as the king's cup bearer. This king was the most influential king in the world and for Nehemiah to be his cup bearer was a great responsibility. This was because the enemies of the king would try and poison him and his job was to stop that from happening. It is equivalent today to the personal assistants of the president of the United States.

When Nehemiah was asked by the king how he could help him, it mentions in passing that: "with a prayer to the God of heaven, I replied…" (Nehemiah 2: 4-5). It is obvious that this prayer was a small, silent prayer before he opened his mouth to answer the king.

We need to remember that his request of the king was not at all logical. He was asking the king that one of the countries in his dominion would be permitted to build a wall which means to have some degree of independence. Such a request could have cost Nehemiah his life, not to mention a lot of persecution to the people of Israel as a result.

Many of us who work in different corporate jobs and are entrusted with many vital decisions each day that affects the lives of thousands of people, can look at Nehemiah as an example of the use of short silent prayers to the God of heaven before we make these decisions.

When Moses was leading the Israelites out of Egypt, directly before the crossing the red sea, he told his people, "The Lord will fight for you, and you shall hold your peace" (Ex 14:14). The sentence after this reveals God talking to Moses saying: "Why are you crying out to me?" (Ex 14:15). This verse has no introduction or reference to Moses saying anything. Many of the church fathers commented on Moses' silence to be a prayer of the heart, which is louder than any audible prayer. St Jerome said: "The word cry in the scripture does not refer to the cry of the voice but to the cry of the heart. In fact, the Lord says to Moses, "Why are you crying out to me?" when Moses had not muttered any cry at all."

Imagine Moses is standing in front of four hundred thousand people all accusing him of leading them into the desert to die. I am sure many people in the corporate world had a similar experience, being blamed for things that are not their fault or out of their hand. You might not have half a million people attacking you, but you have high powered executives at your throat trying to shift the blame on you. We see in the case of Moses, that while he was standing in front of many people encouraging and leading them through a disaster, he had God before him, and he was lifting his heart to Him in silent prayer. Moses' groaning was a strong prayer that was heard by God alone.

These examples of silent prayer that we just read are not examples of a constant prayer of some formula but this is exactly the point I am trying to make. That prayer can have different shapes and forms and we should not limit it to a specific practice. They are not examples of constant prayers, but they show that this person has a strong connection with God especially during the most demanding times, which, in itself, is a prayer.

Being Prayer

The problem still stands, how can someone who has an office job that requires his/her mental concentration to apply this bible command. It is not possible to be repeating a short prayer in mind while trying to read a report or write an email. Asking this question assumes a common misconception about prayer; that it is something you say or do rather than something you are.

In Christianity, prayer is a state of being where the person praying is in the presence of God. Therefore, constant prayer is being in the perpetual presence of God no matter where you are or what you are doing. Thus, being in the presence of God does not necessary require words as much as it requires actions. It is a mode of communication that requires presence but does not require words.

It is the unanimous teaching of the church fathers that what you do as a Christian is a prayer. As early as the second century, St Ignatius of Antioch teaches: "even those things which you do according to the flesh are spiritual; for you do all things in Jesus Christ" (Ephesians 8:2b). St Basil goes as far as saying: "The presence of good works is a louder voice before God." Origen, one of the early Christian writers explains the command to pray without ceasing this way:

> "For the only way we can accept the command to 'pray constantly' (1 Thess. 5: 17) as referring to a real possibility is by saying that the entire life of a Christian taken as a whole is a single great prayer. What is customarily called prayer is, then, a part of this prayer"

St Clement of Alexandria:

> His [the Christians'] sacrifices are prayer, and praise, and readings in the Scriptures before meals, and psalms and hymns during meals and before bed, and prayers again during the night... while engaged in walking, in conversation, while in silence, while engaged in reading and in works according to reason, he in every mood prays

In the same vain St Basil also says:

> "Thus how will you pray without ceasing; if you pray not only in words, but unite yourself to God through all the course of life and so your life be made one ceaseless and uninterrupted prayer."

Abba Lucius, one of the desert fathers was once visited by a group of monks who claimed that they do not do manual labour so as to fulfill the bible verse to pray without ceasing. Abba Lucius asked them if they prayed while they were eating or sleeping to which they replied: no they couldn't. The old man then explained to them the way he fulfils this commandment, saying:

> ...while doing my manual work, I pray without interruption. I sit down with God, soaking my reeds and plaiting my ropes, and I say, "God have mercy on me..." so he asked them if this were not prayer and they replied it was. Then he said to them, "so when I have spent the whole day

working and praying, making thirteen pieces of money, I put two pieces outside the door for anyone in need and I pay for my food with the rest of the money. He who takes the two pieces of money prays for me when I am eating and when I am sleeping. That is how, by God's grace, I fulfil the precept to pray without ceasing"

Therefore, our whole life as Christians is a prayer. When we practice virtue and obey the biblical commandments, we are in fact praying. Throughout the day, there are undoubtedly many opportunities to accomplish this. No matter how busy your life is or how mentally demanding your job is, there is always the chance to obey your parents or partner; there is always a chance to accept being falsely accused of wrong; show love to someone you don't know or dislike; be honest when everyone at work is dishonest; witness to Jesus by our actions; forgive someone who clearly wronged you. By being aware of Gods commandments and striving to fulfill them in your everyday life, you are unwittingly finding yourself in the constant presence of God and therefore, praying without ceasing.

Prayer Techniques

We often narrow down prayer to what we do in our bedroom or prayer corner in the morning or at night before going to sleep. Yet, as we discussed, there are many ways we can left our hearts up in prayer in the workplace.

Spending Time In Nature

We all know the feeling we get once we go into a church. That feeling of stillness that comes from the many prayers that take place in this sacred place. The endless liturgies, psalms and personal prayers gives the church this unmistakable feeling once you go in. Some people have similar experiences sitting down in nature or by a stream of running water. Something I started to appreciate more and more since our monastery is in the middle of the bush. The reason for feeling still while sitting in nature as you would in sacred space is because in nature everything continually praises the Lord. We know from the book of psalms that the trees, snow, birds, animals, all praise the name of the Lord. As a consequence, sitting in nature is like sitting in church where there are constant prayers.

Not everyone is as fortunate as I am to live in the bush. Most of us work in an office space. This, however, does not negate the fact that you can look outside the window. There are numerous studies that support the fact that a simple exercise such as looking outside the window a few times a day will improve your mental heath and performance at work.

Thanksgiving

"Rejoice always, pray without ceasing, in everything give thanks; for this is the will of God in Christ Jesus for you." 1 Thessalonians 5:16-18

In the same verse where St Paul commands us to pray without ceasing, he also commands us to "in everything give thanks". Like he emphasised prayer to be without ceasing, he also emphasised that thanksgiving should be "in everything," meaning in every aspect of our lives. The practice of giving thanks in everything was a common practice of the Jewish prayer life during the first century.

We know from Jewish practices from the first century and earlier, that there were specific short prayers that a faithful Jewish person should recite throughout the day. These prayers are called *berakhah* or blessings. Each of these prayers start with the phrase, "Blessed are you, O LORD our God, King of the universe" and followed by a specific prayer. These prayers were a way of thanking God for different daily activities. While the use of the prayer was flexible, by the second century there were hundreds of prayers every devout Jew was required to pray throughout the day.

Typically in the first century, one would be woken up by the rooster's crow, in which case one should say, "Blessed are you, O LORD our God, King of the universe who hast given the cock intelligence to distinguish between day and night" When dressing: " . . . who clothes the naked". When stepping upon the ground: " . . . who spreads forth the earth above the waters". When putting on shoes: " . . . who hath supplied me with every want." Even when one goes to the toilet ". . . who has formed man in wisdom and created many orifices and vessels, upon the opening or closing of which life depends." This practice was so widespread, to the extent that a person who does not say his prayers before or after meals is looked at as a heathen.

These prayers of thanksgiving were not only limited to experiences of joy and good health, but also during severe trials since we are called to love the Lord with *all* of our hearts. This instruction is not limited to the part of our hearts that are healthy and joyful but also with those that are sad and angry.

In the twentieth century, Pope Kyrillos VI uses similar advice to a young man to use small prayers throughout the day:

> "when you awake, do not remain in bed. Make the sign of the cross on your face, and say, 'in the name of the Father, the son, and the Holy Spirit, one God. Amen. Glory be to the Father, the Son, and the Holy Spirit. Glory be to You, now and forever. Amen'. Then stand up and pray, 'Our Father, who art in heaven…'"

He then continuous to advise the young man to start the day with a prayer of thanksgiving:

> "after that go and wash your face, and stand before God and thank Him for watching over you this night, and keeping you alive until the morning. Pray to Him to protect you this day."

And on his way back from work to:

> "pray in your heart "Lord take care of me; hide me under the shadow of your wings. Oh, my Lord Jesus Christ deliver me from offenses"

When he is back home, he advises the young man to spend quiet time in nature:

> "go outside, far from noise, and ponder the works of the Creator and the beauty of nature. Thank and praise the Lord"

In a sermon by Pope Shenouda III about Fr Mekhail Ibrahim, who was the pope's confession father before becoming a monk, he explains how prayer permeated every step of his life. Every step he took was preceded by the sign of the cross and a short prayer. He would do this before he opens the door of his apartment, before he went down the stairs, when he sat down and even before he opened his mouth to speak.

There is another contemporary saint by the name Fr Bishara, who served at the church of St Mary in the suburb of le Maadi. He was ordained to the priesthood at the age of sixty-five and lived until the age of ninety. It is said by some people who were very close to him that one-day, Virgin Mary appeared to him at church and asked him if he needed anything. Imagine yourself in his situation. You finally have the ear of the Virgin Mary, you can ask anything for yourself, your family, or even the congregation you are serving. However, his reply was astounding as he said: "Tell your Son he has not left me in need of anything." His request to Virgin Mary was thanksgiving for what he has. This spontaneous reaction of thanksgiving can only be explained by the fact that his whole prayer life was made up of thanksgiving.

Therefore, the possibility of achieving continuous prayer is there and we have many saints, not only monks or solitaries but also laymen and married priests with families who serve a large congregation, as an example to inspire us to make our life as a praying presence. Not necessarily to be always saying a prayer, but to live in the presence of God during every aspect of our daily lives, even the most stressful.

CHAPTER 04

PRAYING PAST THE SMOKE

The struggle to pray is real. It is as real for us as it was for all the desert fathers and saints who came before us. Amma Syncletica, one of the desert mothers describes our struggle to pray in this way:"In the beginning, there are a great many battles and a good deal of suffering for those who are advancing towards God and afterwards, ineffable joy. It is like those who wish to light a fire; at first they are choked by the smoke and cry, and by this means obtain what they seek, as it is said: "Our God is a consuming fire" [Heb. 12.24]: so we also must kindle the divine fire in ourselves through tears and hard work."

This sentiment perfectly describes our struggle to pray. We try and try but we don't persist long enough for our prayer to become a consuming fire that consumes our heart. Our experience of prayer is often the smoke and the crying that we experience at the beginning after many failed attempts to get into the habit of praying. Over time we associate praying with smoke and crying, which discourages us from trying again. Subsequently, we ignore the transformative power of being in God's presence in prayer.

There is perhaps no better place to see this transformative power than in the event of the transfiguration of Christ on Mount Tabour. The story begins with Jesus going up to the mountain *to pray* with Peter, James and John. Therefore, the story links prayer with transfiguration. It is in prayer that God reveals himself to us and we are transformed into His image.

Additionally, we read in the Old Testament that Moses, after spending time on the mountain after receiving the commandments, appeared as though, "the skin of his face shone while he talked with Him" (Ex 34:29). Again, forming a relationship between our prayer, or speaking to God, and our transfiguration or our transformation.

In the New Testament, St Paul compares the Jews who could not look at the face of Moses, with us in the New Testament. We, who through prayer have direct access to God in prayer, "beholding as in a mirror the glory of the Lord," and by spending time with God in prayer we are "being transformed into the same image from glory to glory" (2 Cor 3:18).

There is a very interesting story in the *Sayings of the Desert Fathers* that reveals to us how they understood the transfiguration that occurs when we stand up to pray:

> "Abba Lot went to see Abba Joseph and said to him, 'Abba, as far as I can I say my little office, I fast a little, I pray and meditate, I live in peace and as far as I can, I purify my thoughts. What else can I do?' Then the old man stood up and stretched his hands towards heaven. His fingers became like ten lamps of fire, and he said to him, 'If you will, you can become all flame.'"

Stories like this may be discouraging when we read them as they have the capacity to make us question if we are even praying. However, there are three things we need to consider that gives us hope:1- When Jesus was transfigured, He was not alone. The gospels mention that there were "two men" with Him, as if to say that He did not want to be alone when He is glorified but wanted to share this glory with us, human beings. So, it is God's pleasure that I am transfigured with Him 2- These two men were Moses and Elijah, both of which did not have a perfect past. Moses killed the Egyptian and Elijah lost all faith in God and feared Jezebel. Both of which we can identify with, as they did not have the best start to their spiritual lives.3- The two people who appeared with him are Moses and Elijah, one married with a family and a huge responsibility of leading people in the wilderness and the other a "monk" who lived most of his life alone in the desert. Therefore, this transformation is for the monks as much as it is for anyone with a family and responsibilities.

4- Moses, when he came down from the mountain, did not know that his face was shining. The Bible says, "Moses did not know that the skin of his face shone while he talked with Him" (Ex 34:29). So, it is not for us to see our progress in prayer, "our faces shining," but it is for others to see.

Thus, in retrospect, when we develop this habit of prayer, it secretly works in us from glory to glory that will only be seen by others. The only task at hand, is to pray past the smoke.

www.ingramcontent.com/pod-product-compliance
Lightning Source LLC
Chambersburg PA
CBHW031935080426
42734CB00007B/693